OAHU, HAWAII Travel Guide 2023: Where to Stay, What to Do, Eat, For A Perfect Island Getaway

A Bucket List of 100+ Must-See Sites and Hidden Gems on the Island and in Honolulu & Waikiki

Melania Cafaro

Copyright

Copyright ©

Table Of Contents

Oahu Island

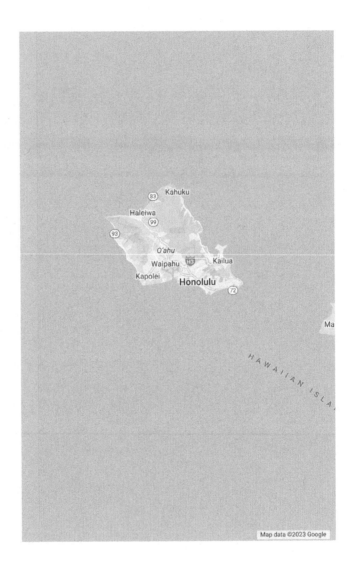

Introduction

Aloha Oahu! Welcome to Oahu

Once upon a time, there was an island paradise in the middle of the Pacific Ocean. This island was called Oahu, and it was a place of breathtaking natural beauty, vibrant culture, and warm hospitality.

Visitors came from all over the world to experience the magic of Oahu – to walk along its white sand beaches, hike through its lush rainforests, surf its legendary waves, and immerse themselves in its rich history and culture.

But navigating this paradise could be overwhelming, especially for first-time visitors. With so many things to see and do, where does one begin? That's where this travel guidebook comes in.

In the pages that follow, we'll take you on a journey through Oahu's most iconic attractions, as well as its hidden gems and off-the-beaten-path destinations. We'll introduce you to the island's diverse neighborhoods and offer insider tips on where to stay, what to eat, and how to make the most of your time on Oahu.

So, if you're an adventure seeker, a history buff, a foodie, or simply seeking a relaxing getaway, Oahu has something for everyone. So pack your bags, grab your sunscreen, and get ready to experience the magic of Oahu – the ultimate island getaway.

History and Geography

Travel back in time to an era long before the arrival of Europeans, and you'll find Oahu thriving with native Hawaiian people. They called it "The Gathering Place" and lived in harmony with the land and sea. Fishing, farming, and gathering were integral to their daily way of life.

But fast forward to 1778, and Captain James Cook and his crew landed on Oahu, marking the island's first contact with the Western world. Over the following years, traders, whalers, and missionaries arrived on Oahu, bringing with them new technologies, customs, and religions.

In the 1800s, Oahu became a bustling hub for the sugar industry, with vast plantations covering much of the island's landscape. Japanese immigrants also arrived on the island, playing a pivotal role in the growth and development of the sugar industry.

During World War II, Oahu became a crucial military base for the United States. The attack on Pearl Harbor on December 7, 1941, marked a turning point in the war and in Hawaii's history. Today, visitors can pay their respects to the lives lost at the USS Arizona Memorial.

But Oahu is more than just a history lesson. It's one of the eight main islands in the Hawaiian archipelago, boasting a total land area of around 600 square miles. From the towering volcanic peaks of the Ko'olau Range to the pristine beaches of the North Shore, Oahu's diverse landscape is a sight to behold.

The island is home to a range of ecosystems, including rainforests, wetlands, and coral reefs. Visitors can explore these unique environments through activities like hiking, snorkeling, and wildlife watching.

Understanding the rich history and geography of Oahu will help visitors gain a deeper appreciation for the island's culture and natural beauty. From ancient Hawaiian roots to modern-day tourism, Oahu's complex history continues to shape the island's identity today.

Getting to Know the Island

Oahu is divided into many diverse zones, each of which has its particular character and attractions. Here are some of the notable neighborhoods in Oahu:

Waikiki

Waikiki is a well-liked tourist site on the island's southern shore. Waikiki is the ideal location to experience the finest of Oahu's metropolitan amenities thanks to its internationally renowned beach, upscale shopping, and exciting nightlife. If you're seeking a more sedate retreat, you might want to look elsewhere because it can get pretty crowded.

North Shore

The North Shore of Oahu is a surfing hotspot that you won't want to miss. Some of the most renowned surf breaks in the world, including Pipeline and Sunset Beach, can be found along this section of the coast.

A peek of Oahu's rustic beauty will be found in the unhurried towns of Haleiwa and Waialua, which are home to several farm-to-table eateries and regional craftspeople.

Kailua

On the windward side of the island, Kailua is a relaxed beach town that attracts both locals and tourists. Kailua provides a less hectic alternative to Waikiki's bustling with its natural beaches, hiking paths, and hip eateries.

Downtown Honolulu

If you have an interest in history and culture, you must visit this area. Several of Oahu's most significant landmarks, such as Iolani Palace, the State Capitol, and the Honolulu Museum of Art, are located in this region. In addition to the renowned. Chinatown, the region is home to a variety of eateries and shops.

East Oahu

The eastern portion of the island is renowned for its breathtaking beaches, dense jungles, and picturesque roads. Water sports enthusiasts frequently visit the village of Hawaii Kai, and the neighboring Koko Crater Trail offers a strenuous climb with stunning scenery.

When to Visit

For the Beach Bum

If your perfect vacation involves lounging on sandy beaches, soaking up the sun, and swimming in crystal-clear waters, then pack your bags for Oahu's summer months from June to August. With temperatures hovering around 85°F (29°C) and minimal rainfall, you'll have plenty of time to perfect that golden tan.

For the Nature Lover

If you're a fan of hiking, exploring rainforests, and spotting wildlife, then spring and fall are your seasons to shine. Cooler temperatures and fewer crowds make these shoulder seasons ideal for experiencing Oahu's natural beauty. Just don't forget your rain jacket if you're visiting in the spring!

For the Culture Vulture

History buffs and culture enthusiasts, listen up! The winter months from December to February are the perfect time to visit Oahu. This is when the island celebrates various cultural festivals and events, such as the Honolulu Festival and the Chinese New Year celebrations in Chinatown.

For the Surfing Enthusiast

Surfs up, dude! Oahu's North Shore is legendary for its massive waves, making it a surfer's paradise. The best time to catch the big swells is during the winter months from November to February.

For Honeymooners and Romantic Getaways

For honeymooners seeking a more romantic and serene vibe, we recommend visiting during the low season from April to early June or September to mid-December. During these months, the crowds are thinner, and you can bask in the island's relaxed and intimate atmosphere. The weather is also delightful, with temperatures ranging from the mid-70s to mid-80s Fahrenheit.

For Families With Kids

Families with young ones, don't fret! Summer break is the perfect time to take the kids to Oahu. The months of June to August offer tons of family-friendly activities and events, such as the Honolulu

Zoo's summer concert series and the Hawaii Children's Discovery Center. The weather is also perfect for outdoor fun, with temperatures ranging from the mid-80s to the low 90s Fahrenheit.

But keep in mind, prices for accommodations and activities may be higher during this peak tourist season. Spring break in March and winter break in December are also excellent options for family fun. So pack those bags and get ready for an unforgettable adventure on the stunning island of Oahu!

Chapter 1

Practical Information

Planning Your Trip

Getting To Oahu

The Daniel K. Inouye International Airport, the island's well-connected international airport, makes it pretty straightforward to get to Oahu from other areas of the world. It acts as a hub for several airlines, providing direct and connecting flights to significant cities all over the world.

Currency

Hawaii's official currency is the US dollar, which makes traveling there simple for Americans. However, if you are a visitor from other parts of the world, it's best to exchange your money before you leave because exchange rates at hotels and airports sometimes aren't advantageous.

Visa Requirements

In terms of visa requirements, US citizens do not need a visa to visit Hawaii, but foreign travelers might. Nonetheless, the majority of tourists to Hawaii are covered by the US visa waiver program, which enables citizens of a select few nations to travel or conduct business in the US without a visa.

Passport

All travelers to Hawaii must possess a current passport, and it's imperative to carry a copy of your passport as well as any other relevant documents with you at all times.

Vaccinations

Although Hawaii does not require vaccinations for entry, it is still a good practice to be current on your usual vaccines before traveling. It's also crucial to take into account any immunizations unique to travel that may be required for your particular schedule. For instance, COVID-19 vaccinations.

Transportation options

Car Rentals

Driving is one of the most well-liked and practical ways to move about Oahu. Rental cars are easily accessible at the airport and other points of the island, allowing you to discover Oahu's hidden gems at your speed. Plan your routes and travel times appropriately, but keep in mind that Oahu traffic may be fairly heavy, especially during peak hours.

Car Rental Options

1. Avis Car Rental

Avis is a well-liked option for tourists thanks to its extensive fleet and handy pick-up and drop-off sites. They provide SUVs and premium cars in addition to tiny, mid-size, full-size, and economical cars.

2. Budget Car Rental

Another well-known rental car agency, Budget provides affordable rates and a selection of vehicles, including small, full-size, and SUVs/vans in addition to economy, compact, and full-size automobiles. They have numerous pick-up and drop-off points all across Oahu as well.

3. Enterprise Rent-A-Car

Enterprise is a reputable option for renting a car, providing a variety of vehicles and top-notch customer service. They have numerous locations on the island of Oahu, including one right at the airport, and provide choices such as small, full-size, and economy automobiles as well as SUVs and trucks.

4. Hertz Car Rental

Hertz has a reputable reputation and a sizable clientele on Oahu. They provide a variety of automobiles, including tiny, full-size, and economical cars, SUVs, and high-end models. They also feature a number of accessible pick-up and drop-off points.

5. Thrifty Car Rental

Thrifty is an affordable option for renting a car, providing cheap rates and a selection of cars, including small, full-size, and SUVs and vans. They have many pick-up and drop-off areas in Oahu.

Public Transport

The "**TheBus**," Oahu's public transportation system, is a cost-effective and effective choice for people who prefer to unwind while traveling. TheBus offers a great way to discover Oahu's attractions, beaches, and cultural sites with over 100 routes covering the entire island. Guests can pay per ride with cash or a reloadable card or buy day, weekly, or monthly passes for unlimited rides.

Bikes

Consider hiring a bike or using a bike-sharing program if you want to see Oahu in a more scenic and environmentally responsible way. As the island's bike trails and lanes continue to grow, they provide a secure and fun opportunity to experience the natural beauty up close. Additionally, renting a bike is generally inexpensive, and many bike-sharing organizations include flexible rental options, such as hourly and daily prices.

Water Transportation

Several ferry and water taxi services run between Honolulu, Waikiki, and different adjacent islands for people who want to explore Oahu's waterways. The coastline, beaches, and secret coves of Oahu can all be explored using these services in a novel and fascinating way.

Safety Tips

Ocean Safety

While the water may seem calm and pleasant, it can be dangerous because of the rip tides and strong currents that can quickly sweep swimmers out to sea.

- Check the weather and surf conditions as well as any posted warning signs or advisories before getting in the water.
- It's important to stick in places approved for swimming and to stay away from going too far out if you're a novice surfer or swimmer.

Hiking Safety

Due to their high inclines, uneven terrain, and potential for bad weather, hiking paths can be difficult.

- Research the trail and its degree of difficulty before starting a hike.
- You should also pack the right clothing, water, and any other supplies you might need.
- It is a smart idea to make someone aware of your whereabouts and anticipated return time.

General Safety Tips

- Theft and other types of petty crime can happen in some places, it's necessary to be aware of your surroundings and keep a watch on your possessions.
- It's a good idea to take care of yourself by drinking enough water,

using sunscreen, and not overdoing it when it's hot outside.

Weather and Climate Information

Oahu has a tropical climate with moderate temperatures and high humidity throughout the year because of its location in the center of the Pacific Ocean.

The dry season runs from May to October, and the wet season runs from November to April. These are the island's two main seasons. You can anticipate pleasant, sunny weather with little to no rain during the dry season. On the other hand, the rainy season provides lower temperatures and more frequent rainfall.

In addition to these seasonal variations, Oahu's location also has an impact on its climate. The island contains a variety of microclimates, thus the weather will change depending on where you are on the island.

For instance, Oahu's North Shore tends to get more rain and cooler weather than the South Shore.

It's crucial to take the weather into account while organizing your vacation to Oahu and how it can affect your travel plans. The dry season, when you may enjoy warm and sunny weather, may be the greatest time to visit if you intend to spend most of your time outside. Yet, traveling during the wet season can provide lower hotel rates and fewer crowds if you are seeking a more affordable vacation.

No matter when you travel to Oahu, it's crucial to dress appropriately for the weather. Pack weather-appropriate attire, such as light, breathable clothing for warm temps and rain gear for the rainy season.

Visitors should be aware of the possible health hazards related to the climate in Oahu in addition to packing appropriately. Dehydration and heat exhaustion can result from the hot and humid weather, especially for people who are not used to it.

It's crucial to stay hydrated by drinking lots of water and avoiding alcohol and caffeine, both of which can cause the body to become even more dehydrated. Also, visitors should be aware of the possibility of mosquito-borne diseases like dengue fever and the Zika virus and take the necessary precautions to stay safe.

Cultural Norms and Etiquette

One of the most important cultural norms in Oahu is the concept of "aloha." Aloha is more than just a word; it is a way of life. It represents love, kindness, and respect for all people, regardless of their backgrounds or beliefs. Visitors to Oahu are encouraged to embrace the spirit of aloha and to treat others with kindness and respect.

The importance given to family and community is another significant component of Oahu culture. Families frequently get together on Oahu for festivities and meals, and guests are frequently welcomed into these get-togethers with open arms. Respecting the island's natural resources and soil is particularly crucial because many inhabitants regard them as sacred.

There are a few things to note when it comes to etiquette. For instance, it is courteous to take your shoes off before entering someone's home, and pointing with your finger is frowned upon. Whenever you are visiting places of worship or going to cultural activities, you are expected to dress modestly.

Money-Saving Tips and Budgeting Advice

1. Plan your trip during the off-peak season, which usually falls between mid-April and early June, as well as from September to mid-December. During these times, flights and accommodations tend to be much cheaper than during the peak tourist season, which is from December to March and from June to August.

2. Consider staying in vacation rentals or guesthouses instead of traditional hotels. Not only are these options often less expensive, but they also offer a more authentic and personalized experience of the local culture.

3. Oahu is home to a variety of food trucks, which offer delicious and affordable local cuisine. Additionally, it's worth checking out the local farmers' markets for fresh produce and other locally sourced goods, which can be used to prepare meals in your vacation rental or guesthouse kitchen.

4. If you plan on visiting multiple attractions during your trip, consider purchasing an attraction pass, which can provide significant savings on admission fees. For example, the Go Oahu Card offers discounted admission to more than 30 of Oahu's top attractions, including Pearl Harbor, the Polynesian Cultural Center, and the Honolulu Zoo.

5. Finally, it's important to be mindful of your spending throughout your trip. Set a daily budget and stick to it, avoiding impulse purchases and unnecessary expenses.

Chapter 2

Where to Stay on Oahu

Top Hotel and Resort Options

The Kahala Hotel & Resort

A 5-star paradise nestled on a private beachfront. With breathtaking views of the Pacific Ocean, a dolphin lagoon, multiple restaurants, and a spa with traditional Hawaiian treatments, this place is a dream come true.

Four Seasons Resort Oahu at Ko Olina

A peaceful retreat on the west coast of Oahu. With four pools, a private beach, and stunning ocean views, this 5-star resort is perfect for a romantic getaway or a family vacation.

Halekulani

If you're looking for an iconic hotel experience, Halekulani is the place for you. With over a century on the Waikiki beachfront, this elegant hotel offers world-class dining options, breathtaking views of Diamond Head and the Pacific Ocean, and luxurious accommodations.

Aulani, A Disney Resort & Spa

For a family-friendly option, Aulani, A Disney Resort & Spa, has got you covered. Featuring Disney-inspired rooms, multiple pools, a lazy river, and activities for kids of all ages, this resort is sure to make your family vacation a magical one.

The Royal Hawaiian

The Royal Hawaiian, also known as the "Pink Palace of the Pacific," offers luxurious accommodations, beachfront activities like snorkeling and surfing, and multiple dining options.

The Ritz-Carlton Residences, Waikiki Beach

If you're looking for apartment-style accommodations with ocean and city views, The Ritz-Carlton Residences, Waikiki Beach is the place to be. This 5-star hotel also features a world-class spa and a rooftop infinity pool.

Turtle Bay Resort

For a more laid-back vacation experience, Turtle Bay Resort on the North Shore of Oahu is the perfect spot. With access to two stunning beaches, multiple pools, and activities like golf and horseback riding, this resort is the ultimate escape from city life.

Prince Waikiki

On the edge of the Ala Wai Harbor, Prince Waikiki offers modern accommodations, multiple dining options, and a 27-hole championship golf course with stunning views of the marina and the Pacific Ocean.

Moana Surfrider, A Westin Resort & Spa

For a historic Hawaiian charm combined with modern amenities, Moana Surfrider, A Westin Resort & Spa, is a must-visit. Known as the "First Lady of Waikiki," this resort offers beachfront activities, multiple dining options, and a luxurious spa.

Andaz Maui at Wailea Resort

Although not on Oahu, Andaz Maui is worth the short flight. This stunning resort offers spacious rooms with ocean views, multiple infinity pools, and access to some of Maui's most beautiful beaches and scenery.

Best Neighborhoods for Different Types of Travelers

The Aqua Ohia Waikiki

A great choice for travelers on a tight budget. With features like a pool and a restaurant on site, this hotel provides tidy, comfortable rooms at a fair price.

The Aston Waikiki Circle Hotel

Offers comfortable accommodations and breathtaking ocean views, which is another excellent option.

The Queen Kapiolani Hotel

A great choice if you're looking for something a little more upscale. With features like a rooftop pool and bar, this recently renovated hotel offers chic and contemporary lodging at an affordable price.

The Kaimuki District

The Kaimuki district is a great choice for visitors who want to see Oahu from a more local perspective. A wide range of eateries, stores, and cafes are available in this developing neighborhood, along with some fantastic lodging options that are reasonably priced.

Paniolo Hale

A charming bed and breakfast with reasonable rates and a welcoming atmosphere and a fantastic choice.

Manoa Cottage

Manoa cottage is a private vacation rental with a cozy ambiance and convenient access to the area's many attractions is another excellent option.

The Kahumana Organic Farm & Cafe

This place is a special choice that provides inexpensive lodging in a stunning natural setting if you're looking for something a little more rustic. In addition to dining on fresh, organic food at the on-site cafe, visitors can stay in cozy cottages or rooms in the main lodge.

Kapolei Area

The Kapolei area is an excellent choice for tourists who want to enjoy a little luxury without going overboard. Some of Oahu's most fashionable and reasonably priced lodgings can be found in this contemporary planned community.

The Hampton Inn & Suites

A fantastic option, offering large, contemporary rooms at a great rate, along with extras like a pool and fitness center.

The Embassy Suites by Hilton Oahu Kapolei

Provides chic suites and lots of on-site amenities, so it is another excellent choice.

The Backpackers Vacation Hotel and Plantation Village are two low-cost lodging choices for families and lone travelers. While Plantation Village has large rooms and a pool, the Backpackers

Vacation Hotel is close to the beach and provides complimentary breakfast.

Vacation Rental Options

Ko Olina Beach Villas

The Ko Olina Beach Villas are luxurious accommodations situated on the sunny west side of Oahu. They offer spectacular ocean views and access to a private beach, making it the perfect getaway for families and groups who want to enjoy resort amenities like a spa and fitness center.

Waikiki Beachside Hostel

The budget-conscious traveler can find affordable and comfortable accommodations at this hostel in the heart of Waikiki. With its prime location, guests have easy access to shopping, dining, and entertainment.

The Diamond Head Beach Hotel & Residences

This is a boutique hotel and vacation rental that boasts beautiful views of Diamond Head and the Pacific Ocean. With modern amenities and a convenient location, it's the perfect retreat for exploring the island.

Hale Koa Estate

The Hale Koa Estate is a luxurious vacation rental in Kailua that blends traditional Hawaiian design with modern amenities. With its private pool and access to Kailua

Beach, families and groups can enjoy a relaxing vacation.

Manoa Valley Inn Bed & Breakfast

For a serene and peaceful retreat, this historic estate in the lush Manoa Valley offers spacious accommodations and stunning gardens.

Hawaiian Princess Oceanfront Condo

The Hawaiian Princess Oceanfront Condo on the west side of Oahu is a modern vacation rental with stunning views of the Pacific Ocean and access to a private beach. With its convenient location, it's the perfect home base for exploring the island.

Kahala Beachside Estate

This is a luxurious beachfront rental that provides the ultimate vacation experience with its spacious accommodations, private pool, and stunning ocean views.

Hale Kai Oceanfront Condominiums

Hale Kai is a charming vacation rental in Lanikai that offers a blend of modern amenities and traditional Hawaiian culture. Its convenient location and traditional design make it a unique and unforgettable experience.

Aston Waikiki Banyan

The Waikiki Banyan, located in the heart of Waikiki, offers affordable and comfortable accommodations with resort amenities like a pool and tennis courts. Its prime location and modern amenities make it the perfect home base for exploring the island.

Unique Accommodations

The Koke'e State Park Cabins

Stay in one of the park's cabins for a primitive and off-the-grid experience. These cottages provide a tranquil getaway for nature enthusiasts, being surrounded by thick trees and offering breathtaking views of Waimea Canyon.

Sunset Beach Treehouse Bungalow

In Sunset Beach, live out your childhood fantasies by booking a stay in a seaside treehouse. This eco-friendly hotel is ideal for couples or lone travelers because it has a private deck and breathtaking ocean views.

Hale Kai

Stay in a Hale Kai, a traditional Hawaiian hut composed of natural materials like thatch and bamboo, for a real Hawaiian experience. This unusual lodging, which is situated on a farm in the verdant Waipio Valley, provides a window into the way of life and culture of the neighborhood.

Kualoa Ranch

Renowned for its breathtaking vistas and appearances in Hollywood movies like Godzilla and Jurassic Park, Kualoa Ranch has a variety of unusual lodging options, including glamping tents and log cabins.

Participate in a variety of outdoor activities like horseback riding and ATV trips while seeing the valley's natural splendor.

Volcano House

While staying at Volcano House in Hawaii Volcanoes National Park, you can witness the grandeur and strength of the state's active volcanoes. This historic hotel offers once-in-a-lifetime views of the Kilauea Caldera and evening lava glow.

Kauai Beach Resort

Stay at Aqua Kauai Beach Resort for an environmentally friendly resort experience. This resort makes use of sustainable practices like solar power and water conservation. Relax in a plush hotel or suite while taking advantage of the resort's beachside setting.

Bellows Field Beach Park Campsite and Cabins

On Oahu's east coast, on a stunning stretch of beach, these cabins offer a distinctive camping experience with all the conveniences of a home. This lodging is ideal for families and groups because it offers a choice of cabin sizes with beachfront access.

Camp Mokule'ia

A nonprofit retreat center that provides a range of lodging alternatives like yurts and cottages, Camp Mokule'ia offers an eco-friendly and community-focused experience. This unusual lodging is ideal for outdoor enthusiasts and wildlife lovers, with a focus on sustainability and outdoor education.

Hawaiian Sanctuary Retreat Center

The Yurt Village at Hawaiian Sanctuary offers a distinctive glamping experience with all the conveniences of home. It is situated on the island's lush and tropical east side. This lodging is ideal for individuals looking for a tranquil and environmentally friendly escape because it offers a range of yurt sizes and features like a yoga studio and farm-to-table restaurant.

Chapter 3

What to Do on Oahu

Top Attractions

Diamond Head State Monument

You'll be rewarded with expansive vistas of the island as you ascend to the top of Diamond Head. This volcanic crater is a must-see destination because it provides breathtaking views of the Pacific Ocean and the city below.

The Pearl Harbor National Memorial

This attraction is a memorial to the sailors and soldiers who lost their lives in the attack on Pearl Harbor. It is a location of great historical significance. The USS Arizona Memorial offers tours so that visitors can learn more about the occasions that led to America's involvement in World War II.

Waikiki Beach

This is one of the most well-known beaches in the world, and it is noted for its distinctive surf. It's the ideal location to unwind and enjoy the sun thanks to its white beach and crystal-clear waters.

Hanauma Bay Nature Preserve

An ideal location for snorkeling and scuba diving. It is also a protected marine life conservation area. Tourists can explore the various coral reefs and get up-close views of tropical fish.

Kualoa Ranch

This working cattle ranch on the eastern side of Oahu is also a popular setting for Hollywood productions. Guests can take a guided tour of the grounds to see some of the well-known film locations, including the Jurassic Park set.

Manoa Falls

A short journey through a tropical jungle is required to reach this impressive waterfall, which is situated in the verdant Manoa Valley. Visitors can see the waterfall's beauty up close by following the trail to its base.

Iolani Palace

Iolani Palace is an important historical location in Hawaii because it is the only royal residence in the country. A guided tour of the palace is available for those who want to learn more about the final Hawaiian Kingdom kings and queens.

North Shore Beaches

Oahu's North Shore is renowned for having some of the world's largest waves, which visitors may catch at locations like Sunset Beach and Pipeline. Also, it's a terrific spot to unwind and experience the laid-back island attitude.

Byodo-In Temple

Situated in the Valley of the Temples Memorial Park, this magnificent temple is a reproduction of a 900-year-old temple in Japan. The tranquil grounds are open for visitors to meander through while they take in the beautiful structure.

The Polynesian Cultural Center

This center is a wonderful resource for learning about local traditions and customs because it celebrates Polynesian culture. Guests can take part in a variety of cultural activities, witness a hula dance performance, and enjoy a traditional luau.

Bishop Museum

This is the biggest in Hawaii and is devoted to preserving and promoting Hawaiian history and culture. There is something for everyone to appreciate, from exhibits of ancient antiquities to modern art.

Makapuu Lighthouse Trail

This beautiful trail takes tourists to the top of a cliff where they can see the Makapuu Lighthouse and the Pacific Ocean. The area is beautiful all year round and is excellent for whale watching in the winter.

Outdoor Activities

Surfing

Surfing is a well-liked pastime in Oahu because of the island's reputation for having world-class surfing locations. Beginners should head to Waikiki Beach, while advanced surfers should go to the North Shore.

Hiking

Oahu provides a variety of hiking trails for hikers of all experience levels thanks to its lush rainforests and gorgeous mountain ranges. Diamond Head hike leads to the top of a dormant volcano and provides stunning vistas across the island.

Snorkeling

Oahu is the ideal location for snorkeling due to its crystal-clear waters. Hanauma Bay is a well-liked location for snorkeling and provides a close-up view of the abundant marine life on the island.

Scuba Diving

Scuba diving is a must-do activity in Oahu if you want a more intense underwater experience. A popular diving location that provides a window into Hawaii's maritime past is the Sea Tiger wreckage.

Stand-Up Paddleboarding

Using a stand-up paddleboard to explore Oahu's waterways is entertaining and relaxing. Kailua Beach is a fantastic place for beginners because of the calm waves there.

Kayaking

Kayaking is a well-liked method of discovering Oahu's waterways. A fantastic place to launch your kayak and see the stunning Mokulua Islands is the Lanikai Pillboxes trek.

Horse Rides

Enjoy a leisurely ride across the verdant landscape of Oahu. Guided excursions via picturesque paths and meadows are available at the Gunstock Ranch in Kahuku.

Cycling

Cyclists love Hawaii for its picturesque roads and mountain paths. Bike riders can enjoy a scenic path through a verdant rainforest on the Manoa Falls trail.

Zip-lining

Fly through the forests of Oahu to get your heart racing. You can take zip-lining trips through the rainforest's treetops at the Coral Crater Adventure Park.

Parasailing

Fly over Oahu's crystalline seas to get a bird's-eye perspective of the island. At Waikiki, parasailing is a well-liked pastime that provides breathtaking views of the island's shoreline.

Golfing

With breathtaking vistas of the ocean and mountains, Oahu is home to some of the world's most stunning golf courses. The Ko Olina Golf Club is a well-liked hangout for golf fans.

Fishing

Oahu is an excellent place to go fishing because of its rich marine life. Deep-sea fishing is popular along Hawaii's Waianae Coast, where there's a chance to catch some of the state's biggest fish.

ATV Tours

ATV tours are a must-do activity in Oahu if you're looking for an exhilarating off-road adventure. The Kualoa Ranch ATV rides transport you through lovely valleys and gives you a taste of the island's illustrious past.

Helicopter Tours

Take a helicopter tour to see Oahu from a unique angle. The journey passes via some of the island's most beautiful sights, such as the North Shore and the Diamond Head crater.

Camping

Immersing yourself in Oahu's natural beauty while camping is a terrific way to have a unique outdoor experience. The beach in Malaekahana is relatively uncrowded compared to other beaches on the island. This is because it is situated in a more remote location, away from the hustle and bustle of the tourist areas. Visitors to this beach can enjoy the peace and quiet and take in the natural beauty of the surroundings.

For those looking to stay near Malaekahana Beach, there are a few options available. The Malaekahana Beach Campground is a popular choice for those looking for a rustic camping experience. The campground offers tent sites and cabins, as well as basic amenities such as restrooms and showers.

Cultural Experiences

Visit a Luau

A traditional Hawaiian luau is a must-do during any trip to Hawaii. Enjoy live music, hula dancing, delicious Hawaiian food and drinks, and more while getting to know the community.

Where to go: Alii Luau at the Polynesian Cultural Center, Germaine's Luau, or Paradise Cove Luau.

Check out the Bishop Museum

A top-notch museum that highlights the natural history and culture of Hawaii and the Pacific is the Bishop Museum. For people who want to learn about the history of the islands, then visit Bishop Museum in Honolulu.

Discover the history of Hawaiian traditions

Cultural institutions can be found all across the island where you can learn about old Hawaiian customs including hula dance, lei making, and traditional Hawaiian games. The best places to learn Hawaiian history include the Waikiki Aquarium, Hawaii

Plantation Village, and the Polynesian Cultural Center.

Visit the Iolani Palace

The Hawaiian Kingdom's official house, Iolani Palace, is now a museum that chronicles the kingdom's history. It's a fantastic location to discover the island's lengthy history. Iolani Palace is in Honolulu's central business district.

See a Traditional Hawaiian Dance Performance (Hula)

Hawaii's national dance is the hula, and you can watch hula performances all around the island.

Visit the Polynesian Cultural Center, Waikiki Aquarium, and Waikiki Beach Walk.

Explore Chinatown

A distinctive fusion of cultures and cuisines may be found in Honolulu's Chinatown, a lively and historic area. Visit the area's numerous stores, eateries, and galleries.

Visit The Hawaii State Art Museum

A beautiful museum in Honolulu that displays both modern and traditional Hawaiian art. The local art scene can be discovered there in great detail.

Attend a Traditional Hawaiian Music Concert

Listen to the lovely sounds of traditional Hawaiian music festivals and concerts throughout the island.

You can visit a concert at Hawaii Theatre Center, Waikiki Shell, or Blue Note Hawaii.

Visit the Pearl Harbor National Memorial

For history aficionados, the Pearl Harbor National Monument is a must-see. Visit the USS Arizona Monument to learn more about what happened on December 7, 1941, and pay your condolences.

Stroll Through The Honolulu Museum of Art

One of the biggest and most complete art museums in the nation is the Honolulu Museum of Art. It exhibits a wide range of artwork from different cultures, including numerous works created by regional artists.

Take a Trip to the Waikiki Aquarium

A stunning aquarium that displays the marine life of Hawaii and the Pacific. It's a fantastic location to discover the neighborhood ecosystem.

Take a farm Tour

Learn about the island's farming and culinary traditions by taking a visit to a nearby farm. Visit Kahumana Organic Farms.

Beaches and Water Sports

Waikiki Beach

One of Oahu's most renowned beaches located in the heart of Honolulu. This world-famous sandy stretch is celebrated for its warm waters, stunning sunsets, and vibrant ambiance. Waikiki is also a hub for thrilling activities, such as surfing, stand-up paddleboarding, and snorkeling, making it a perfect destination for families, couples, and solo travelers.

North Shore

Another favored beach destination which is home to some of the world's most iconic surf breaks, including Pipeline and Sunset Beach. The North Shore is a haven for both surfers and beach lovers, offering numerous opportunities for relaxation and reflection in its serene bays and gorgeous beaches. During the winter months, adrenaline junkies can take advantage of the waves that can reach up to 30 feet.

Lanikai Beach

A hidden gem hidden away in the charming town of Kailua, perfect for travelers seeking a more private experience. This unspoiled beach boasts powdery white sands and turquoise waters, providing a peaceful setting for a romantic sunset stroll or a calm picnic. Adventurous travelers can also kayak to the nearby Mokulua Islands for a unique perspective on Oahu's coastline.

Kailua Beach Park

An ideal spot for families with young children. This sheltered beach offers a playground and calm waters, ensuring a safe and enjoyable area for kids to splash and play. The nearby town of Kailua also provides plenty of family-friendly activities such as hiking, shopping, and dining.

Family-Friendly Activities

Visit the Honolulu Zoo

For animal enthusiasts of all ages, a trip to this kid- and family-friendly zoo is a must. There are around 900 animals totaling over 300 species, so there is a lot to see and discover. Also, you can join one of the zoo's many educational programs or enjoy a guided tour.

Go Snorkeling at Hanauma Bay

If your family enjoys the water and its inhabitants, Hanauma Bay is the ideal location. Many fish species and other sea life can be found in this designated marine life conservation area, and the area's crystal-clear waters make snorkeling a breeze. Take a guided snorkeling tour. To beat the crowds, make sure to get there early.

Hike to The Diamond Head

It's one of Oahu's most recognizable sights, and the ascent is truly a once-in-a-lifetime experience. The sights are worth it despite the steep and difficult route. Take a camera, lots of water, and sunscreen with you!

Spend the Day at the Beach

Oahu is home to some of the most stunning beaches on the planet, thus it is a must-do activity for families. With calm waves and lots of amenities, Waikiki Beach is a popular choice, so try Lanikai Beach, with its white beaches and blue waves, if you want somewhere a little quieter.

See the USS Arizona Memorial

The USS Arizona Monument is a must-see attraction for history aficionados. This monument honors the 1,177 sailors and Marines who perished in the Pearl Harbor attack and serves as a somber reminder of the sacrifices made during World War II.

Check out the Polynesian Cultural Center

This live museum displays the history and culture of the Pacific Islands. You can go on a guided tour, take part in a traditional luau, and see cultural displays.

Join a whale-watching tour

If you're visiting Oahu in the winter, a guided tour will allow you to get up close and personal with humpback whales as they migrate to the warm seas off the coast of Oahu each winter to mate and give birth.

Visit the Dole Plantation

The Dole Plantation is an entertaining and instructive destination for families. This pineapple farm has a train ride, a garden maze, and a pineapple garden, among other family-friendly amenities. Explore the largest maze in the world, take a train tour of the plantation, and have a taste of the pineapple delight called Dole Whip or Soft Serve.

Visit the Waikiki Aquarium

For those who enjoy animals, this is a fantastic destination. A wonderful site to learn about Hawaii's distinctive underwater ecosystem. It is a modest but educational aquarium, which features over 500 species of marine animals and plants.

Go on a Horseback Riding Excursion

If you're searching for a more energetic trip, think about going on a horseback riding tour. There are several choices, ranging from straightforward rides for new riders to more difficult courses for seasoned ones.

Visit the Escape Rooms

The Breakout Waikiki Escape Room is a well-liked escape room. The "Island Task Force" room in this escape room is one of several themed rooms where you and your family will be required to solve a mystery involving a missing artifact. Another thrilling option is the "Kamehameha Treasure" chamber, where you and your team will attempt to unravel a mystery involving the fabled King Kamehameha.

The Chambers Escape Games is another excellent choice; it has a variety of themed rooms, like "The Lost Tomb," "The Pirate's Lair," and "The Wild West." The family will have a fascinating experience because there are different tasks and puzzles to complete in each room.

Visit Wet'n'Wild Hawaii

With over 25 rides and activities ideal for people of all ages, Wet'n'Wild Hawaii is one of the most visited places in Oahu. Wet'n'Wild Hawaii offers a variety of attractions for visitors of all ages, from the adrenaline-pumping Tornado and Island Racer to the more laid-back Kapolei Kooler lazy river.

Hawaiian Waters Adventure Park

A water park with several slides, a wave pool, a lazy river, and other attractions. It is situated in Kapolei. Families with children of all ages can have a blast there for the day.

Sea Life Park

Try The Dolphin Encounter, one of the most well-liked attractions which allows visitors to interact closely with these wonderful animals.

Kualoa Ranch

The working ranch Kualoa Ranch offers a variety of excursions and activities that are ideal for families with young children. Everyone will find something to enjoy at

Kualoa Ranch, from horseback riding to zip lining.

Chapter 4

Where to Eat on Oahu

Best Local Cuisine

Poke

Poke is one of Oahu's most widely consumed foods (pronounced poh-kay). This raw fish salad is frequently served as an appetizer or a main dish. Ahi tuna which has been marinated in soy sauce, sesame oil, and aromatic spices like ginger and garlic is used to make the meal. Octopus, shrimp, and even tofu can be used as varieties.

Plate lunch

Plate lunch is another essential component of Oahu cuisine. This traditional Hawaiian dish is served with rice and macaroni salad and often contains a protein like chicken or kalua pork. Since it has gained such popularity, you can get the meal at practically every restaurant on Oahu, and many of them have their own distinctive takes on it.

Laulau

Laulau is yet another age-old Hawaiian delicacy that is popular today. The meal is prepared by encasing fish or pork in taro leaves and baking it in an underground oven. A soft and tasty dish is the end product, which is frequently served with rice and a side of poi, which is produced from mashed taro root.

Malasadas

These donuts with Portuguese influences are a favorite sweet on Oahu and are sold in a lot of neighborhood bakeries. The donuts can be filled with a variety of tastes, including custard, chocolate, or haupia, and are deep-fried and sprinkled with sugar (coconut pudding).

Shave Ice

This cold treat is produced by slicing a block of ice and spreading flavorful syrups over it, frequently in exotic tastes like passionfruit, mango, and pineapple. The outcome is a delightful treat that is excellent on a hot day.

Beverages

Mai Tai

Mai Tai is one of the island's most well-liked local beverages. This traditional Polynesian cocktail is made with rum, lime juice, orange curaçao, and orgeat syrup. Fresh mint and a slice of pineapple are frequently added as garnishes. It has long been a favorite with both natives and visitors in the tropics.

Blue Hawaii

Blue Hawaii is also popular. The bright blue color and sweet, tropical flavor of this cocktail, which is created with blue curaçao, rum, pineapple juice, sweet and sour mix, and occasionally vodka or gin, are its trademarks. This popular beverage, which gained notoriety in the 1950s thanks to the Elvis Presley film of the same name, is now served in bars and eateries all across the island.

Shochu

Try the Shochu if you're searching for something a little less sweet. The alcohol percentage of this Japanese beverage, which is manufactured from sweet potatoes or barley, is a little lower than that of more well-known alcoholic beverages like whiskey or vodka. This adaptable beverage is frequently paired with food and can be served hot or cooled.

Lava Flow

The Lava Flow is another well-known local libation on Oahu. This cool beverage is typically served with a straw to resemble a volcano and is created with rum, coconut cream, pineapple juice, and strawberry puree. It's a colorful and enjoyable beverage that's great for enjoying on a hot day.

Pina Colada

Although this beverage may not be exclusive to Hawaii, it is unquestionably popular there. This traditional cocktail, which is blended or served frozen and contains rum, coconut cream, and pineapple juice, is incredibly sweet and creamy.

Fine Dining Options

La Mer

A Five Star restaurant with breathtaking views of the Pacific Ocean. It is located inside Waikiki's renowned Halekulani Hotel. The eatery is recognized for its exquisite service, modern French food, and opulent setting. Foie gras torchon, lobster bisque, and rack of lamb are just a few of the locally produced delicacies on the menu.

Chef Chai

Chef Chai serves up modern Hawaiian-Asian fusion food. As a James Beard Award-winning chef, Chef Chai has gained recognition for his creative meals that combine tastes from the Pacific Rim. Fresh seafood, sushi, and grilled meats are just a few of the dishes the restaurant serves, all of which are made using materials sourced locally.

Orchids

This restaurant serves traditional Hawaiian dishes that are delicious and filling. The service is amazing and they serve vegetarian-friendly food.

Hidden Gems

Haili's Hawaiian Foods

This inconspicuous eatery in the Kalihi district serves some of the island's greatest traditional Hawaiian cuisine. At Haili's Hawaiian Foods, you will get to sample the authentic tastes of Hawaii, from laulau to poke to kalua pork.

Helena's Hawaiian Food

This Kaimuki neighborhood restaurant is another hidden gem. This family-run restaurant has been providing great traditional Hawaiian fare and has garnered various accolades for it. The pipikaula (beef jerky made in the style of Hawaii) and poi are to die for (mashed taro root).

Giovanni's Shrimp Truck

On the North Shore, one of the most well-known is Giovanni's Shrimp Truck. This food truck, which has been dishing out plates of garlic shrimp for more than 25 years, is a must-stop for visitors visiting Oahu.

Tacos Vicente

With a focus on authentic flavors and fresh ingredients, this food truck offers some of the greatest Mexican cuisines on the island.

Chinatown

Honolulu's Chinatown is the place to go if you want to eat like a local. There are numerous eateries and street vendors here that serve anything from dim sum to pho to shave ice. Ask locals for their suggestions as the food scene in Chinatown is always changing.

Farmers' Markets

Kapiolani Community College Farmers Market

This market is located in Honolulu, close to Waikiki, and it is open every Saturday morning. With over 50 exhibitors selling a variety of fruit, artisanal crafts, and regional delights, the KCC Farmers Market is a hive of activity. Visitors can get everything they need in this place, from homemade baked delicacies to freshly squeezed juices and exotic fruits and veggies.

Haleiwa Farmers Market

The sellers at this market, which takes place every Sunday, offer everything from farm-fresh fruit to handcrafted goods and jewelry. Indulge in some delectable cuisine choices like grilled meats, acai bowls, and fresh poke bowls.

Waimea Valley Farmers Market

This market is hosted every Thursday and is framed by the breathtaking Waimea Valley, which is dotted with tumbling waterfalls and lush tropical plants. You can stroll among the stalls and take in the fresh produce's brilliant colors and scents while listening to live music and entertainment.

Pearlridge Farmers Market

Every Saturday, this market attracts a lot of locals since it has a wide variety of fresh vegetables, baked products, and handcrafted crafts. Guests can peruse the booths while indulging in the aroma of freshly brewed coffee, mingling with friendly vendors, and taking in the neighborhood vibe.

Vegetarian and Vegan Options

Greens & Vines

This fine-dining establishment offers exquisite raw vegan food produced with locally and organically sourced ingredients. A variety of inventive meals, such as zucchini linguine with pesto and sun-dried tomatoes, and avocado and grapefruit tartare, are available on the menu.

Peace Cafe

This is a well-liked vegetarian and vegan eatery on Oahu situated right in the middle of Honolulu. Lentil burgers, vegetable curries, and macrobiotic bowls are just a few of the vegan and vegetarian options available at this small eatery. The cafe also provides organic and gluten-free alternatives.

Best Places for a Romantic Dinner or a Night out With Friends

Roy's

Popular Hawaiian fusion eatery Roy's provides a laid-back and informal setting that's ideal for a night out with friends. Roy's offers a wide selection of dishes that are sure to please any palate with a menu that highlights the best of Hawaiian and Asian flavors. Dessert aficionados must sample the restaurant's famous chocolate soufflé.

Duke's Waikiki

Duke's Waikiki is the ideal choice for a fun and energetic night out. Duke's, a bar with a beachfront location, provides a relaxed atmosphere that's ideal for socializing over drinks and small plates with friends. Duke's is a well-liked destination for both visitors and residents due to its live music and breathtaking ocean views.

Hula Grill Waikiki

Hula Grill is a terrific place for a date or a night out with friends because of its open-air dining space and breathtaking beach views. The cuisine of Hula Grill, which is well-known for its fresh seafood and Hawaiian-inspired meals, is ideal for sharing and trying out different flavors. Check out the restaurant's beverage menu as well; it offers a variety of delectable and inventive drinks that are sure to please.

Chapter 5

Insider Tips and Hidden Gems

Secret Beaches and Hidden Hikes

Makalawena Beach

This beach is found in Kekaha Kai State Park and is one of the most beautiful. The 20-minute hike across difficult terrain to get to this beach is an adventure by itself. The vista of the turquoise oceans and white sand beaches that await you once you get there, however, is breathtaking.

Manoa Falls Trail

The Manoa Falls Trail is another hidden gem; it leads to a stunning waterfall tucked away in a verdant rainforest. Families with kids can do the hike because it's reasonably easy, and it's absolutely gorgeous.

Lanikai Pillbox Trek

The Lanikai Pillbox Trek should be tried if you're up for a more difficult hike. This path leads to several military pillboxes with expansive views of the sea and the surrounding islands.

There are multiple volcanic craters on Oahu, each with its own terrain and past. Diamond Head, which offers a 360-degree panorama of the island from its summit, is one of the most impressive. The Koko Head

Crater Trail, which requires over 1,000 steps to ascend, is another fantastic alternative.

Cultural Events and Festivals

Merrie Monarch Festival (April 9 - April 15, 2023)

The Merrie Monarch Festival, a week-long celebration of Hawaiian culture and art, takes place every year in Hilo on the Big Island of Hawaii. The festival draws thousands of visitors from all over the world and includes hula competitions, art exhibits, and live music performances.

Prince Lot Hula Festival (July)

Honors hula, one of Hawaii's most significant cultural traditions. Live music and dance performances, authentic foods and crafts, and a range of other cultural activities are all part of the festival.

Honolulu Festival (March)

The Honolulu Festival is a three-day celebration of the various cultures of Hawaii and the Pacific Rim that takes place in March. The festival draws guests from all over the world and includes live performances, parades, and cultural exhibitions.

Ukulele Festival

Takes place in July and honors the legendary instrument that has come to be associated with Hawaiian music. Live music performances, workshops, and a range of other cultural events are all part of the festival.

Waikiki Spam Jam (April 30- May 14, 2023)

Spam is a canned meat product that has become a mainstay of Hawaiian cuisine, and the Waikiki Spam Jam is a special occasion that honors this love. Live music, food vendors, and a range of other cultural activities are all part of the festival.

Kamehameha Day Celebration (June 11, 2023)

King Kamehameha, the first king to unify the Hawaiian islands under one kingdom, is commemorated on this state holiday in Hawaii. Parades, live music, and a wide range of other cultural activities are all part of the celebration.

Aloha Festivals

Throughout September, many activities are held to honor Hawaiian culture and heritage. Live music performances, hula contests, and various other cultural events are all part of the festivals.

Lantern Floating Hawaii

Takes place every Memorial Day and is a stunning and heartfelt memorial to those who have died. Each year, hundreds of people attend the festival, which includes a floating lantern ceremony, live music, and other cultural activities.

Off-the-Beaten-Path Attractions

Kaena Point State Park

This is a remote, untamed area that is home to a variety of indigenous plants and animals. It is situated at the westernmost point of Oahu. The park is a wonderful location for trekking and birdwatching.

Shangri La

In the affluent area of Diamond Head, there is a museum that is dedicated to Islamic art and culture which is a hidden treasure. Since Doris Duke, the museum's creator, traveled widely in the Middle East and Asia, she amassed a collection of priceless artifacts from the Islamic world.

Hoomaluhia Botanical Garden

This garden is a calm sanctuary with lush vegetation and a serene lake that is tucked away in a valley on the windward side of the island. There are picnic spots, strolling paths, and a diversity of flora from different parts of the world in the garden.

Makapuu Point Lighthouse Trail

The beautiful Makapuu Lighthouse Trail on the island's east side provides sweeping views of the coastline and the Pacific Ocean. The Makapuu Lighthouse, which has been directing sailors since 1909 can be reached through a trail that ascends to it.

Lanikai Pillbox Hike

The Mokulua Islands and the azure waters of Lanikai Beach may both be seen in stunning detail from the short but strenuous Lanikai Pillbox Hike, which is located on the east side of the island.

Waiahole Poi Factory

Poi, a staple of Hawaiian culture derived from taro, has been produced at the family-run Waiahole Poi Factory for more than a century. Guests can try freshly prepared poi while learning about the cultural significance and history of this popular dish.

Local Shopping and Souvenirs

Aloha Stadium Swap Meet

This marketplace, which takes place every Wednesday, Saturday, and Sunday, is a

MEL'S ADVENTURERS' ALMANAC: Oahu, Hawaii Travel Guide

great venue to shop. More than 400 merchants offer a variety of goods such as handcrafted jewelry, clothes from regional clothing companies, and Hawaiian foods. This market is a fantastic spot to find one-of-a-kind goods and souvenirs while taking in the lively atmosphere of a local market.

Ala Moana Center

The Ala Moana Center is a must-visit if you're looking for upscale retail alternatives. With over 350 shops, this mall offers everything from pricey options like Forever 21 and H&M to luxury labels like Gucci and Chanel. The mall provides a wide range of culinary options in addition to shopping, making it the ideal place to spend an afternoon.

Chinatown

Visit Chinatown neighborhood in the heart of Honolulu if you're searching for a distinctive shopping experience. Many boutiques and businesses can be found in this area, selling everything from handcrafted jewelry to vintage clothing. The region also has some art galleries and museums, making it an excellent place for both shopping and cultural discovery.

The island of Oahu boasts a wide selection of unusual mementos. The Hawaiian shirt, often known as the "Aloha shirt," is a well-liked item and is distinguished by its vibrant and floral patterns. The "haku lei," a kind of flower crown fashioned with live flowers and greenery, is another unusual gift option. These lovely and aromatic crowns can be used as a hair ornament or as a terrific photo opportunity.

Best Places to Catch a Sunset or Sunrise

Sunsets:

Sunset Beach: Popular for its stunning sunsets and big-wave surfing.

Waikiki Beach: Waikiki offers breathtaking sunsets over the Pacific Ocean.

Yokohama Bay: This remote beach on the west side of the island offers a stunning sunset view with the backdrop of the Wai'anae Mountains.

Tantalus Lookout: This scenic overlook located in the lush Pu'u Ualaka'a State Park provides panoramic views of the city and ocean during sunset.

Ko Olina Lagoons: The calm waters of Ko Olina Lagoons provide the perfect setting for a peaceful sunset.

Sunrises:

Makapu'u Point Lighthouse: This Lighthouse offers stunning sunrise views over the ocean.

Lanikai Beach: This picturesque beach on the Windward Coast offers a tranquil sunrise view.

Diamond Head: A unique vantage point for watching the sunrise over the city and ocean.

Waimanalo Beach: This secluded beach on the eastern side of the island offers a peaceful and serene sunrise view with the backdrop of the Ko'olau Mountains.

Sandy Beach: This popular beach offers a unique sunrise experience with the sun rising over the mountains rather than the ocean.

Chapter 6

Useful Travel Phrases

Asking for Directions:

"E kala mai, e ku'u aloha, nani wale keia wahi. Pehea e hiki ia'u ke hele i...?" (Excuse me, my friend, this place is so beautiful. How can I get to...?)

"Aloha, e kala mai, 'eia ke ala e hele ai i...?" (Hello, excuse me, what is the way to get to...?)

"Aloha, 'o wai ka mea nana e hiki ia'u ke hele i...?" (Hello, who can tell me how to get to...?)

Ordering Food:

"E kala mai, e ku'u aloha, hana hou, keia mea ai?" (Excuse me, my friend, can I have another one of this food?)

"Mahalo nui, ua maika'i ka mea'ai." (Thank you very much, the food is excellent.)

"Ke noi aku nei wau i kekahi kope." (I would like to order a coffee, please.)

Health and Emergencies:

"E kala mai, o'u inoa 'o... E hele aku au i ke kauka." (Excuse me, my name is... I need to go to the doctor.)

"E kala mai, e ku'u aloha, he pilikia ko'u mau maka." (Excuse me, my friend, I have a problem with my eyes.)

"Ke noi aku nei wau i kōkua. 'A'ole au i hiki ke hele." (I need help. I can't walk.)

Common Everyday Phrases:

"Aloha kakahiaka" (Good morning)

"Aloha 'auinalā" (Good afternoon)

"Aloha ahiahi" (Good evening)

"A hui hou" (See you later)

"Mahalo" (Thank you)

"E 'olu'olu" (Please)

"Aloha" (Hello/goodbye/love)

"Mele Kalikimaka" (Merry Christmas)

"Hau'oli Makahiki Hou" (Happy New Year)

Conclusion:

A Comprehensive Bucket List of 100+ Must-See Sites and Hidden Gems on Oahu

- ☐ Book for a Go- City Pass, an all-inclusive pass featuring 40+ attractions and tours.
- ☐ Take a Hop- On Hop- Off bus tour of Honolulu, a fun way to see all of the city.
- ☐ Go on a guided parasailing tour of the island.

☐ Book for a Waikiki Atlantis submarine adventure and see Waikiki under the sea.

☐ Take a sunset cruise on a catamaran.

☐ Enjoy a couple's massage at a luxurious spa.

☐ Take a private surf lesson with your partner.

☐ Enjoy a romantic dinner at a beachfront restaurant

☐ Take a helicopter tour of the island.

☐ Watch the sunrise at Makapuu Point.

☐ Take a scenic drive to the North Shore.

☐ Enjoy a beach picnic at Lanikai Beach.

☐ Take a couples photography session at a scenic location.

- ☐ Go horseback riding at Kualoa Ranch.
- ☐ Attend a traditional Hawaiian luau.
- ☐ Go on a snorkeling excursion.
- ☐ Visit the Honolulu Museum of Art.
- ☐ Take a hike to the top of Diamond Head.
- ☐ Attend a sunset hula show.
- ☐ Take a sunset sail on a yacht.
- ☐ Have a romantic picnic at Puu Ualakaa State Park.
- ☐ Go on a private helicopter tour of the island.
- ☐ Take a scenic drive to the Koko Head Crater.
- ☐ Take a romantic walk along Waikiki Beach.
- ☐ Take a surf lesson at Waikiki Beach.

☐ Hike to the top of the Stairway to Heaven.

☐ Explore the Ala Moana Center shopping mall

☐ Take a stand-up paddleboarding lesson at Kailua Beach

☐ Visit the USS Arizona Memorial at Pearl Harbor.

☐ Go on a whale-watching or dolphin watching tour.

☐ Take a hike to the Manoa Falls.

☐ Attend a traditional Hawaiian hula show.

☐ Explore the Hawaii State Art Museum.

☐ Take a scuba diving excursion.

☐ Take a surf lesson at Waimea Bay.

☐ Explore the Honolulu Chinatown.

- ☐ Take a snorkeling excursion to Hanauma Bay.
- ☐ Take a guided tour of the USS Missouri at Pearl Harbor.
- ☐ Take a sunset hike to the top of the Diamond Head.
- ☐ Take a hike in the Hanauma Bay Nature Preserve.
- ☐ Visit the Nuuanu Pali Lookout for breathtaking views of the island.
- ☐ Take a guided tour of the Waimea Valley Botanical Garden.
- ☐ Take a bike tour of the North Shore.
- ☐ Visit the Manoa Heritage Center for a historical and botanical tour
- ☐ Take a guided hike in the Makiki Valley Loop Trail.

☐ Visit the Diamond Head State Monument and hike to the top.

☐ Take a kayak tour to the Mokulua Islands.

☐ Take a trip to Pu'u 'Ualaka'a State Park (Tantalus Lookout) for beautiful views and instagrammable pictures.

☐ View Mokoli'i (Chinaman's hat) from Kane'ohe bay and Kualoa regional Park.

☐ Explore Lyon Arboretum, a free botanical garden adjacent to Manoa valley.

☐ Take a tour of He'eia fishpond, a historic fish pond located at He'eia State park and learn about the modernized technology of seafood harvesting.

☐ Visit the USS Arizona Memorial at Pearl Harbor.

☐ Explore the Pacific Aviation Museum.

☐ Visit the Iolani Palace, the official residence of Hawaii's last monarchs.

☐ Visit the Hawaii State Capitol Building and take a guided tour.

☐ Take a historical walking tour of Honolulu's downtown.

☐ Visit the National Memorial Cemetery of the Pacific.

☐ Explore the Bishop Museum and its exhibits on Hawaiian history and culture.

☐ Visit the Pearl Harbor Aviation Museum.

☐ Take a guided tour of the historic Dole Plantation.

☐ Take a food tour of Honolulu's Chinatown

☐ Visit the Honolulu Night Market for food and drinks

☐ Have a poke bowl at Ono Seafood

☐ Visit the KCC Farmers Market for fresh local produce and food vendors

☐ Have shave ice at Matsumoto Shave Ice

☐ Visit the Kahuku Farms for farm-fresh food and smoothies.

☐ Take a food tour of the North Shore's shrimp trucks and food stands.

☐ Have a malasada from Leonard's Bakery.

☐ Try the garlic shrimp at Giovanni's Shrimp Truck.

☐ Visit the Waialua Sugar Mill for locally made chocolates and coffee.

☐ Go skydiving with Skydive Hawaii or other available sky diving tours.

☐ Take a jet ski tour of Oahu's coast.

☐ Go parasailing off Waikiki Beach.

☐ Take a zip line tour of the Kualoa Ranch.

☐ Go on a shark cage diving excursion.

☐ Take an ATV tour of Kualoa Ranch.

☐ Go on a jet boat tour of Oahu's coast.

☐ Take a free-dive or scuba-diving excursion.

☐ Go on a bungee jumping adventure with Banzai Bungee Hawaii.

☐ Visit the Byodo-In Temple, a replica of a 900-year-old temple in Kyoto, Japan.

- ☐ Hike the Kuliouou Ridge Trail, a challenging 5-mile hike with panoramic views of the east side of Oahu.

- ☐ Explore the Manoa Falls Trail, a 1.6-mile hike that leads to a beautiful 150-foot waterfall.

- ☐ Go on a shark cage dive tour with North Shore Shark Adventures.

- ☐ Visit the Hawaii State Art Museum to see a collection of contemporary Hawaiian art.

- ☐ Take a surf lesson with the Hans Hedemann Surf School.

- ☐ Visit the Honolulu Museum of Art to see a collection of Asian, Hawaiian, and Western art.

☐ Explore the Hawaii State Capitol building and take a tour of the Senate and House chambers.

☐ Take a sunset sail with Hawaii Nautical and watch the sun dip below the horizon.

☐ Visit the Iolani Palace, the only royal palace in the United States.

☐ Go on a horseback riding tour of the island with Gunstock Ranch.

☐ Visit the Waikiki Aquarium to see a collection of marine life native to Hawaii.

☐ Explore the USS Arizona Memorial at Pearl Harbor to learn about the history of World War II.

☐ Take a day trip to the neighboring island of Kauai to see the stunning Waimea Canyon.

☐ Visit the Lyon Arboretum, a 200-acre botanical garden with over 5,000 species of tropical plants.

☐ Take a stand-up paddleboarding lesson with the Hawaii Surf Lessons.

☐ Visit the USS Bowfin Submarine Museum & Park to learn about the history of submarines and see a real World War II submarine.

☐ Take a yoga class at the Yoga Floats studio, where classes are held on stand-up paddleboards.

☐ Visit the Makapuu Lighthouse Trail for stunning views of the Pacific Ocean and the eastern coast of Oahu.

☐ Go on a kayaking and snorkeling tour of Kaneohe Bay with Kama'aina Kayak & Snorkel Adventures.

☐ Take a cooking class with Hawaiian Style Cooking to learn how to make traditional Hawaiian dishes.

☐ Explore the Diamond Head State Monument, a popular hiking trail that leads to a scenic lookout.

☐ Visit the Pearlridge Center, one of the largest malls in Hawaii, for a shopping and dining experience.

☐ Take a sunset dinner cruise and enjoy a 7-course meal while watching the sunset.

☐ Visit the National Memorial Cemetery of the Pacific, also known as the

Punchbowl Cemetery, to pay respects to veterans.

☐ Go on a deep-sea fishing tour.

☐ Explore the Koko Crater Botanical Garden, a unique garden located inside a dormant volcano.

☐ Take a day trip to the neighboring island of Maui to see the famous Road to Hana.

☐ Visit the Foster Botanical Garden, a 14-acre garden with over 10,000 species of tropical plants.

☐ Visit the Hawaii State Library, the largest library in Hawaii, and take a tour of its unique architecture.

For Families with Kids:

☐ Visit the Waikiki Aquarium

☐ Take a kid-friendly snorkeling tour at Hanauma Bay.

☐ Explore the Honolulu Zoo.

☐ Visit the Children's Discovery Center.

☐ Take a beach day at Ko Olina Lagoon.

☐ Visit the Hawaii Children's Discovery Museum.

☐ Go on a pirate-themed snorkeling excursion with Hawaii Pirate Ship Adventures.

☐ Visit the Dole Plantation for train rides and a giant maze.

For Sports Enthusiasts:

☐ Take a surf lesson at Waikiki Beach.

☐ Play a round of golf at one of Oahu's many courses.

☐ Go on a snorkeling or scuba-diving excursion.

☐ Take a hike to the top of Diamond Head.

☐ Attend a University of Hawaii football game.

☐ Play beach volleyball at Ala Moana Beach Park.

☐ Go on a kayaking excursion.

☐ Rent bikes and explore Oahu's scenic bike paths.

☐ Take a stand-up paddleboard lesson.

☐ Visit the Hawaii Polo Club and watch a match.

For Relaxation

☐ Take a yoga class on the beach at sunrise or sunset.

☐ Visit the Lomi Lomi Spa for traditional Hawaiian healing treatments.

☐ Take a dip in Waikiki Beach or Kailua Beach.

☐ Visit the Byodo-In Temple for a peaceful and meditative experience.

☐ Take a sound healing or crystal healing session.

☐ Go on a forest bathing walk at Ho'omaluhia Botanical Garden.

☐ Take a sunset sail along Oahu's coast.

☐ Visit the Waimanalo Beach Park for a quiet and serene beach experience.

☐ Try a float tank session at Dream Float Hawaii.

☐ Take a hot stone massage at Moana Lani Spa.

Final Thoughts

As the sun sets on your adventures in Oahu, we hope that this travel guidebook has served as your trusty companion, guiding you through the rich and diverse experiences that the island has to offer. From the breathtaking natural beauty of its beaches and landscapes to the vibrant cultural experiences, thrilling family-friendly activities, and exquisite dining options, Oahu has truly captivated your senses and left you with unforgettable memories.

We hope that this book has not only provided you with practical information but has also sparked a sense of wonder and curiosity within you, inspiring you to explore and discover even more of the island's hidden treasures on your own. As you continue your journey through life, may the spirit of aloha and the warmth of the Hawaiian people stay with you always, reminding you of the beauty and joy that can be found in every moment.

Thank you for allowing us to be a part of your Oahu adventure. And remember to always ask the locals for the best recommendations, explore the city on your own and always have a map handy. There are many audio tours and guided tours available too, if that is what you prefer, so choose one that suits you.

We wish you safe travels and many more exciting journeys ahead. Aloha!!!

Made in United States
Orlando, FL
18 April 2023